D1232376

All Around Ohio

Regions and Resources

Marcia Schonberg

Heinemann Library
Chicago, Illinois

www.heinemannraintree.com
Visit our website to find out
more information about
Heinemann-Raintree books.

To order:

☎ Phone 888-454-2279
💻 Visit www.heinemannraintree.com
to browse our catalog and order online.

©2003, 2010 Heinemann Library
an imprint of Capstone Global Library, LLC
Chicago, Illinois

Edited by Megan Cotugno
Designed by Ryan Frieson, Kim Miracle, Betsy Wernert
Photo research by Tracy Cummins
Originated by Heinemann Library
Printed in China by Leo Paper Products Ltd.

13 12 11 10 09
10 9 8 7 6 5 4 3 2 1

New edition ISBNs: 978-1-4329-2569-7 (hardcover)
                   978-1-4329-2576-5 (paperback)

Library of Congress Cataloging-in-Publication Data
Schonberg, Marcia.
  All around Ohio / Marcia Schonberg.
    p. cm. -- (Heinemann state studies)
Summary: Provides a look at Ohio's different geographical
regions and the industry and economy of each.
Includes bibliographical references and index.
  ISBN 1-4034-0665-0 -- ISBN 1-4034-2688-0 (pbk.)
  1. Ohio--Geography--Juvenile literature. 2.
Regionalism--Ohio--Juvenile literature. [1. Ohio--Geography.]
I. Title.
II. Series.
  F491.8.S36 2003
  917.71--dc21   2002154202

Acknowledgments

The author and publishers are grateful to the following
for permission to reproduce copyright material: **p. 4**
Americanspirit Royalty-Free/Inmagine; **pp. 21, 24B, 27B,
31T, 39T** Robert Lifson/Heinemann Library; **p. 28** Tom
Uhlman; **pp. 5, 6, 9, 11, 13, 19, 20, 29, 30, 32, 36, 43, 45**
maps.com/Heinemann Library; **p. 7** NASA/Roger Ressmeyer/
Corbis; **p. 10** Mark C. Burnett/Photo Researchers; **p. 12** Susan
Spetz/Image Finders; **p. 13** Bill Kiskin; **p. 14** Karen Schaefer/
WCPN; **p. 15** Sauder Woodworking Company; **p. 16** Shaker
Heights Public Library Local History Collection; **p. 17T** John
Sohlden/Visuals Unlimited; **p. 17B** courtesy of Libbey Glass;
p. 18 NASA/John Glenn Research Center; **p. 22** aceshot1/
Shutterstock; **pp. 23, 33** Jim Baron/Image Finders; **p. 24** Bryan
Busovicki/Shutterstock; **p. 25** Corbis; **p. 26T** Andy Snow;
p. 27T Jeff Greenberg/Visuals Unlimited; **p. 31B** Bohemian
Nomad Picturemakers/Corbis; **p. 35** J.D. Pooley/Getty
Images; **p. 37** David Muench/Corbis; **p. 38** Tom McNemar/
Shutterstock; **p. 39C** Chris Crook/Zanesville Times Recorder;
p. 39B Doug Sokell/Visuals Unlimited; **p. 40** Bettmann/Corbis;
p. 41 U.S. Forest Service-Wayne National Forest; **p. 44** Kevin
R. Morris/Corbis

Cover photograph of Old Man's Cave, Hocking Hills Region,
Ohio, reproduced with permission of ©Doug Lemke/
Shutterstock.

Contents

Some words are shown in bold, **like this**. You can find out what they mean by looking in the glossary.

Ohio's Geography

Ohio is located in the Midwestern United States. It is the state farthest east in this region. Ohio is often called a **Great Lakes** state, because a Great Lake—Lake Erie—serves as Ohio's northern border.

An imaginary line through the middle of Lake Erie is the **political boundary** that lies between the United States and Canada. The Ohio River runs along the southern boundary of Ohio. It was made the southern boundary when Ohio was carved out of the **Northwest Territory** and became a state in 1803. The Ohio River marks the border between Ohio and West Virginia, and between Ohio and Kentucky. Three other states share borders with Ohio, too.

Ohio attracted settlers more than 200 years ago. They came in search of land and jobs. If you ask today's Buckeyes, a nickname for people who live in Ohio, you will learn that many of them live in Ohio because of the land and jobs, too. They also live there because of the climate and way of life. In fact, more than eleven million people call Ohio home. Ohio is the seventh most populated state in the nation.

To find out more about Ohio's population, see the map on page 30.

People know they have crossed the border from other states into Ohio because of signs like the one pictured above.

4

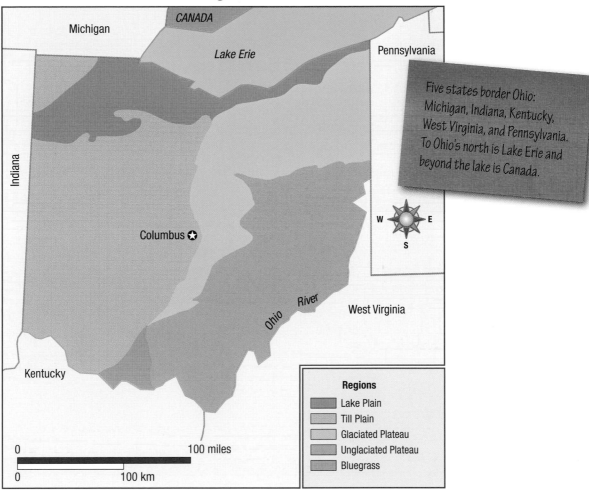

The Five Regions of Ohio

CANADA

Michigan

Lake Erie

Pennsylvania

Indiana

Columbus ✪

Ohio River

West Virginia

Kentucky

Five states border Ohio: Michigan, Indiana, Kentucky, West Virginia, and Pennsylvania. To Ohio's north is Lake Erie and beyond the lake is Canada.

W E
S

| 0 | | 100 miles |
| 0 | | 100 km |

Regions
- Lake Plain
- Till Plain
- Glaciated Plateau
- Unglaciated Plateau
- Bluegrass

Landforms

Thousands of years ago, much of Ohio was covered by a large glacier, a huge block of ice and snow more than a mile thick. It was so heavy, so huge, and stayed frozen for so long, that it carved hills and valleys as it slowly moved. As the **climate** became warmer, the glacier retreated northward. It scraped and flattened the land that eventually became northwestern Ohio. More than 10,000 years ago, deep valleys filled with water as the glacier inched its way north and melted at the end of the last **Ice Age**.

The movement of glaciers helped form Ohio's five different land regions. Each of these regions is known for different features. Ohio's five regions are the Lake Plains, Till Plains, Glaciated **Plateau**, Unglaciated Plateau, and Bluegrass. This book discusses the resources found in each region and how they are used by the people living in each region.

Climate

Ohio's **landforms** vary across its different regions. Likewise, the **climate** varies depending on the region. However, across Ohio there are four seasons. Winters are cold and summers are warm. There is more rainfall in the spring and summer than in the fall and winter. Rainfall in spring and summer often includes thunderstorms, and even tornadoes. The average yearly temperature in southern Ohio is 14° Celsius (57° Fahrenheit), while the average temperature in the northeast is 10° Celsius (50° Fahrenheit).

One of the most important features of Ohio's climate is that there is no natural barrier between Ohio and northern **polar** regions. A natural barrier is something, such as a mountain range, which stops weather from moving toward a region. Cold winds from northern Canada are therefore not uncommon in Ohio in the winter.

Ohio Precipitation

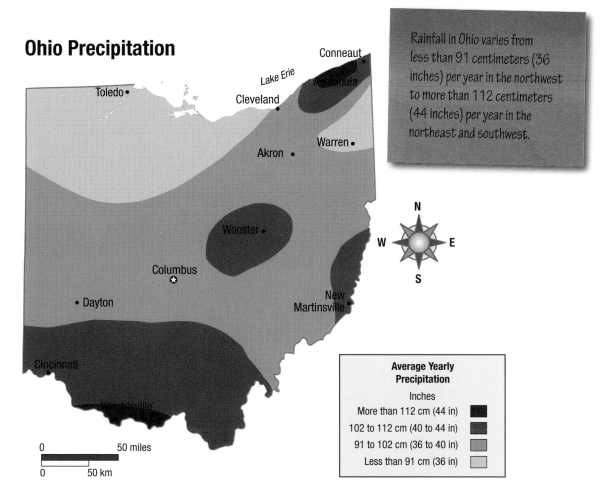

Rainfall in Ohio varies from less than 91 centimeters (36 inches) per year in the northwest to more than 112 centimeters (44 inches) per year in the northeast and southwest.

Conneaut
Lake Erie
Ashtabula
Toledo
Cleveland
Warren
Akron
Wooster
Columbus
Dayton
New Martinsville
Cincinnati
Wrightsville

N
W   E
S

0   50 miles
0   50 km

Average Yearly Precipitation

Inches

More than 112 cm (44 in)

102 to 112 cm (40 to 44 in)

91 to 102 cm (36 to 40 in)

Less than 91 cm (36 in)

Natural Resources

Lakes and rivers play a part in the way Ohio developed long ago and in the way Ohioans work and play today. There are more than 3,300 named rivers and streams in Ohio. There are as many smaller, less significant branches that are not named. There are also more than 60,000 lakes, **reservoirs**, and ponds in Ohio.

During the final melting stages of the Ice Age glacier, about 10,000 years ago, early Native Americans, called Paleo-Indians, made their way into Ohio. They had no maps. They followed the paths of the huge **prehistoric** animals they hunted. The Paleo-Indians became the first people to use Ohio's **natural resources**. They discovered **flint** deposits in Ohio. They used the flint for weapons and tools. The Paleo-Indians killed mastodons, wooly mammoths, and other animals for food. They used the animal skins for clothing and shelter.

Flint is just one of Ohio's many natural resources. Valuable natural resources in Ohio include forests, water, land, and minerals. Natural resources provide materials that people use to make goods. This in turn creates jobs, since people are needed to make goods out of the resources.

Gifts from a Great Glacier

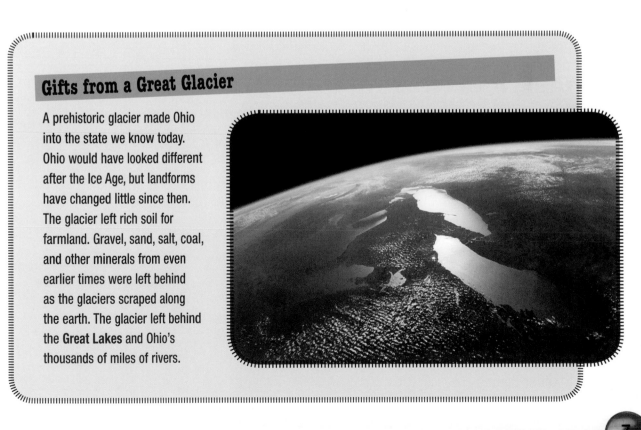

A prehistoric glacier made Ohio into the state we know today. Ohio would have looked different after the Ice Age, but landforms have changed little since then. The glacier left rich soil for farmland. Gravel, sand, salt, coal, and other minerals from even earlier times were left behind as the glaciers scraped along the earth. The glacier left behind the **Great Lakes** and Ohio's thousands of miles of rivers.

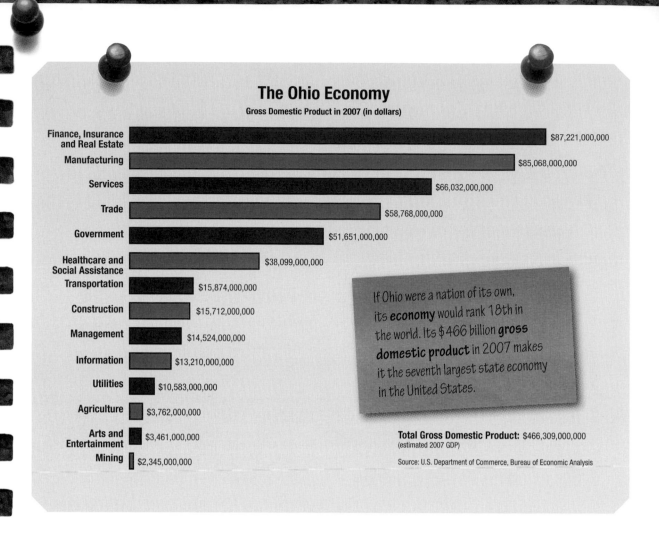

The Ohio Economy

Gross Domestic Product in 2007 (in dollars)

Finance, Insurance and Real Estate	$87,221,000,000
Manufacturing	$85,068,000,000
Services	$66,032,000,000
Trade	$58,768,000,000
Government	$51,651,000,000
Healthcare and Social Assistance	$38,099,000,000
Transportation	$15,874,000,000
Construction	$15,712,000,000
Management	$14,524,000,000
Information	$13,210,000,000
Utilities	$10,583,000,000
Agriculture	$3,762,000,000
Arts and Entertainment	$3,461,000,000
Mining	$2,345,000,000

If Ohio were a nation of its own, its **economy** would rank 18th in the world. Its $466 billion **gross domestic product** in 2007 makes it the seventh largest state economy in the United States.

Total Gross Domestic Product: $466,309,000,000
(estimated 2007 GDP)

Source: U.S. Department of Commerce, Bureau of Economic Analysis

Using Resources

Ohio's **human resources** are the people who turn natural resources into products and goods that people can use. Ohio's economy depends on a number of different **industries**. Many workers in Ohio have jobs in manufacturing. Other Ohioans work in agriculture, forestry, and fishing. They may raise livestock or grow vegetables, which are often used to produce other food products.

The goods and products made in Ohio are sent to more than 200 countries and all over the United States. This is partly due to Ohio's location. Many towns and cities were built near Ohio's waterways. Ohio has other strong transportation routes, such as highways and interstates, which crisscross the state. They provide fast and inexpensive transportation of products made in Ohio to other places.

To find out more about Ohio's transportation, see the map on page 32.

Not all of the goods made in Ohio leave the state. The people living in Ohio use a portion of the products made there. They often use services provided by other Ohioans. Businesses that provide services include restaurants, hotels, health care services, shops, and even computer programming. In Ohio most people work in the service industry. In fact, three out of every four employed Ohioans work in service-related jobs.

To find out more about Ohio's population centers, see the map on page 30.

Ohio Resources

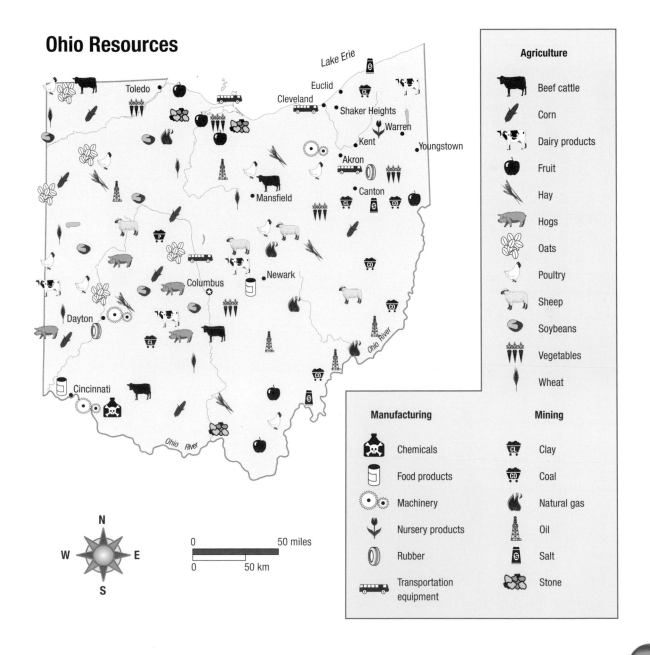

Agriculture
- Beef cattle
- Corn
- Dairy products
- Fruit
- Hay
- Hogs
- Oats
- Poultry
- Sheep
- Soybeans
- Vegetables
- Wheat

Manufacturing
- Chemicals
- Food products
- Machinery
- Nursery products
- Rubber
- Transportation equipment

Mining
- Clay
- Coal
- Natural gas
- Oil
- Salt
- Stone

0   50 miles
0   50 km

Lake Plains

The Lake Plains are the flat stretches of land located in northern Ohio. They lie along much of the southern shore of Lake Erie and stretch to the Ohio borders with Indiana in the west and Michigan in the north. The Lake Plains include plains and sandy beaches along the coast that were once covered by several large glacial lakes.

Lake Erie itself is a product of a great glacier that covered the area. The huge block of ice dug deep holes in the earth's surface, which filled with water as the glacier melted, creating Lake Erie. The Maumee, Huron, Sandusky, and Auglaize rivers feed into Lake Erie. They, too, were formed by narrow grooves left behind by the glacier.

Glacial Grooves State Memorial on Kelleys Island in Lake Erie shows effects from the great glacier that once covered Ohio.

Lake Plains Region

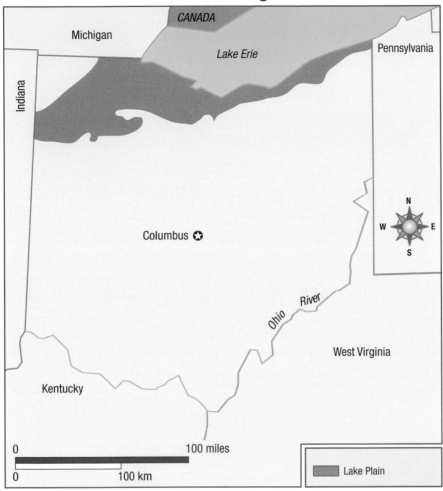

Transportation

Lake Erie is the most important **natural resource** in the Lake Plains. One reason Lake Erie is so important to the region is because it links with other lakes and rivers. Before road and rail travel existed, this network of waterways connected Ohio with other states on the East Coast. It was Ohio's transportation system for many years and was a key reason why people settled in Ohio. It allowed the state to ship products made in Ohio to other parts of the world. From Lake Erie, ships could travel east through Lake Ontario, then onto the St. Lawrence River and into the Atlantic Ocean.

Because of Ohio's location along this important trade route, the Lake Plains remains a **densely** populated part of the state. Lake Erie is important to the people who live in the region. People continue to depend on Lake Erie for jobs, **recreation**, and transportation.

Lake Erie forms most of the northern border of Ohio. Its coast runs for 502 kilometers (312 miles) in the state, from Toledo in the west to Conneaut in the east. Eight important harbors dot the northwestern Ohio shore. The cities of Toledo, Sandusky, and Huron are important to the **economy** in the region because they all have important **ports** on this **Great Lake**.

To locate Ohio's ports, see the transportation map on page 32.

It is easy to reach nearby islands from these ports. Lake Erie has many islands, but only a few where people live year-round. One way to get to the islands is by **ferryboat**. These boats leave from Sandusky and other ports and head to Put-in-Bay, the Bass Islands, and Kelleys Island. These Lake Erie islands are included in the Lake Plains region.

This region also includes inland lakes and city and state parks for camping, hiking, and other types of recreation. The Cleveland Lakefront State Park runs along Lake Erie in downtown Cleveland, and a number of parks dot Lake Erie islands. These parks help the travel and tourism **industry** by attracting visitors to the region.

The Cuyahoga Valley National Park is one of the most visited national parks in the United States.

Kelleys Island is the largest American freshwater island in Lake Erie. It measures 6.4 kilometers (4 miles) by 3.2 kilometers (2 miles) and is a popular destination for tourists.

Most state parks in the Lake Plains are near Lake Erie or on its islands.

Ohio State Parks

Most of the 60,000 to 70,000 tons of salt Cleveland uses to make winter driving less hazardous comes from ancient salt beds under Lake Erie.

Natural Resources

Salt deposits were formed in the Lake Plains 410 million years ago, when Ohio was covered by a warm sea. When the sea gradually dried up, salt deposits were left behind. As a result, Ohio is one of the nation's top producers of rock salt, and the industry employs around 4,000 people there. Four million tons of rock salt are mined each year from mines in Cleveland and Fairport Harbor. These deposits of rock salt, which can be up to 61 meters (200 feet) thick, are located 610 meters (2,000 feet) beneath Lake Erie. Most of the salt is used during Ohio's snowy winters to melt snow on streets and roads.

Lake Erie helps keep the weather in the Lake Plains milder than in other regions in Ohio. Lake Erie breezes can cool a summer day. The lake also helps keep winter days warmer. As a result, the region has a long growing season.

Much of the Lake Plains is covered in a rich soil that is ideal for farming, but it has poor drainage. The soil comes from deposits left by the glacial lakes. Much of this land makes up the northwest part of the Lake Plains, an area called the Black Swamp. Long ago, the land of this area was thought to be of poor quality. A large lake, Lake Maumee, covered the area during **prehistoric** times. Even after the lake dried up, the land was too wet to farm. The Black Swamp was the last part of Ohio to be settled because no one wanted to live there.

Amish and Mennonite settlers began draining the Black Swamp in the mid-1800s. They had the idea of creating farmland from the wetlands. Today, after years of draining and dredging, Ohio's best farmland covers this area. Some people believe it is among the best farmland in the country. A blanket of fertile, black soil gives a whole new meaning to the name Black Swamp. Many descendants of the Amish and Mennonite farmers live in the region today.

Farmers in the Black Swamp raise some unusual crops, such as popcorn, sugar beets, and pickles. But corn and soybeans are the most popular crops. Ohio's largest wheat crops also come from northwestern counties. The Lake Plains, combined with counties in the upper half of the Till Plains region (see page 19), help make Ohio a leading agricultural state.

Often, farmers here have two jobs. More than half of Ohio's farmers who participated in the last agricultural census stated they held other jobs besides farming. This way, farmers can earn extra wages while keeping their farming traditions. Those with small farms often take jobs in manufacturing, yet continue to operate their farms. Some farmers even start their own manufacturing companies.

The Fostoria Flour Mill

Much of the wheat farmed in northwestern Ohio's Lake Plains and Till Plains goes to the Mennel Milling Company in Fostoria. After the soft, red winter wheat is harvested, it is often ground into flour at the company's flour mill. This is one of the few remaining milling companies in Ohio. The milling company's interesting history proves how important location can be to companies in Ohio. Back in 1886, the company's owners built the mill in Fostoria for several good reasons. First, five freight trains rolled through Fostoria and could ship flour across the country. Second, natural gas, one of the area's resources, was available for energy. The City of Fostoria offered the natural gas for free if the mill generated the energy to light the city's streetlamps, a new invention at the time.

A fire destroyed the mill in 1897, but it was rebuilt. Today, it is a modern plant and meets the highest production standards. It is the largest mill in Ohio.

Industry

Erie Sauder, who lived in the Black Swamp, started the Sauder Woodworking Company in the small town of Archbold. Sauder created furniture products known as RTA, or ready-to-assemble. With a few simple tools, almost anyone who can read can put together the furniture at home. The company has 3,500 workers today.

Erie Sauder founded Sauder Woodworking in 1934.

While Ohio's location on Lake Erie first attracted early settlers who farmed or even created new companies, the lake later attracted **industrialists** who were eager to build factories near such a fine source of transportation. Manufacturing, or the process of turning **raw materials** into finished goods, became a major source of jobs. Today, the manufacturing industry employs one million people in Ohio.

Ohio's three most important manufactured goods are transportation equipment, industrial machinery, and fabricated metals. However, manufacturing in the Lake Plains is very diverse. It once supported mainly the steel industry and its related jobs, but the region's residents of today perform many different kinds of work.

Riding the Rapid

There are other forms of transportation besides water that are important to Ohio's Lake Plains region today. One form came as the result of one of the first **suburban** communities in the United States. Two brothers, Oris Paxton and Mantis James Van Sweringen, planned the community called Shaker Heights. Once this area east of downtown Cleveland was built, residents needed a way to get downtown to their jobs. In 1913 the brothers' idea of an electric train, the Shaker Heights Rapid Transit, began service. It ran from Shaker Heights to **Terminal Tower** in downtown Cleveland. The brothers designed the terminal, too.

Today, the Rapid Transit Authority, called the RTA for short, whisks passengers to and from communities surrounding Cleveland. Special high-speed connections make travel from the airport to downtown easy. Sports fans also like to ride the rapid to downtown Cleveland to watch their favorite Ohio sports teams play.

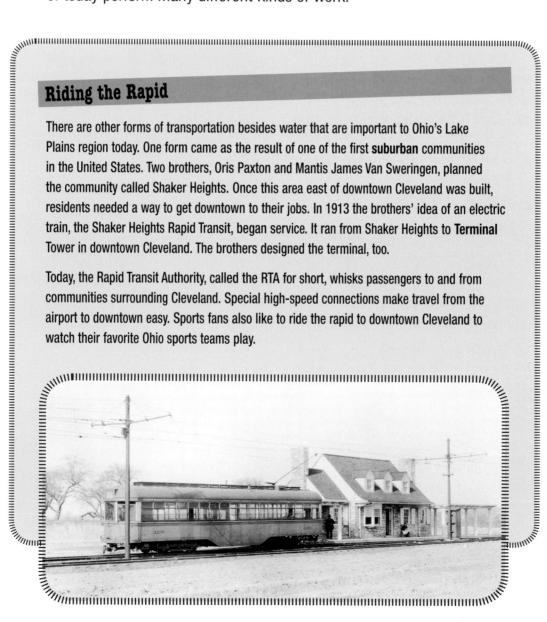

Goods manufactured in the Lake Plains include automobiles and auto parts, appliances, roller bearings, paint and varnish, power wheelchairs, and automatic teller machines (ATMs) used for banking. These goods are shipped from the ports on Lake Erie. Cars manufactured by the thousands of employees of General Motors, the largest nongovernmental employer in Ohio, leave ports in Lorain, Cleveland, Ashtabula, Fairport Harbor, and Conneaut for foreign countries and other cities throughout the United States.

The products made in Ohio are shipped all over the world from Lake Erie ports such as Toledo, pictured here.

In addition to an excellent transportation system, Toledo, like other **prosperous** Ohio cities, has natural resources, such as gas and oil. These important factors drew Edward Libbey and his large glass factory from New England to Toledo. In 1935 the Libbey Glass Factory was bought by the Owens-Illinois Glass Company, which became Owens-Illinois, Incorporated, in 1965. Today the company is owned by Kohlberg Kravis Roberts. Its Libbey Glass Company division still operates at its original site in Toledo. The Libbey factory is a major reason why Toledo became known as the Glass Capital of the World.

Glass production still provides jobs for 2,000 people in and around Toledo.

Glass, auto parts, furniture, dishwashers, and other types of goods are manufactured in and around the Lake Plains. These goods are transported by rail, land, water, and air to other states and countries. Many of these products are grown or manufactured in small, rural communities.

Manufacturing and shipping, however, are not the only important industries in the Lake Plains. Many people there work in the service industry. They work in hospitals, banks, restaurants, shops, or in **high-tech** companies. As home to the Wright brothers, who made the first controlled flight in a powered aircraft, flying has an important history in Ohio. **Technology** combines with Ohio's history as a flight center in places such as **NASA's** John Glenn Research Center at Lewis Field in Cleveland. Opened in 1941, it develops technology and researches better ways to power flight. The center employs 3,500 Ohioans at Lewis Field, next to Cleveland Hopkins International Airport.

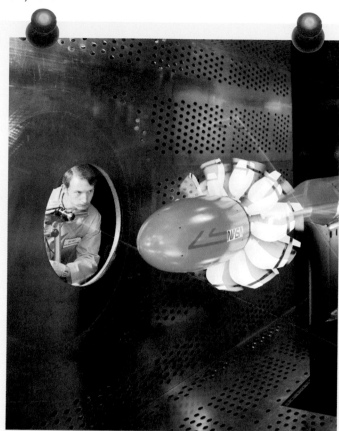

Wind tunnels at NASA's John Glenn Research Center in Cleveland allow researchers to experiment with flying without leaving the ground.

Financial companies also contribute to the Lake Plains economy. One of the 12 Federal Reserve banks in the United States is located in Cleveland. The Federal Reserve is the central bank of the United States that oversees the country's money supply. Other banks, including KeyCorp and National City, have headquarters in Cleveland.

Till Plains

The Till Plains cover most of the western part of Ohio. The last **Ice Age** glacier carved rolling hills and valleys across much of the Till Plains. It carved **gorges**, or deep, narrow grooves, in places such as the Little Miami River, which flows through John Bryan State Park near Dayton, in southwestern Ohio.

Both the highest and lowest points in Ohio are located in the Till Plains. The highest point is called Campbell Hill, in Logan County, near the center of the region. Campbell Hill is 472 meters (1,549 feet) above sea level. Ohio's lowest point is the Ohio River which runs along the state's southern border. It is 132 meters (433 feet) above sea level.

To locate Ohio's highest and lowest points, see the map on page 20.

Till Plains Region

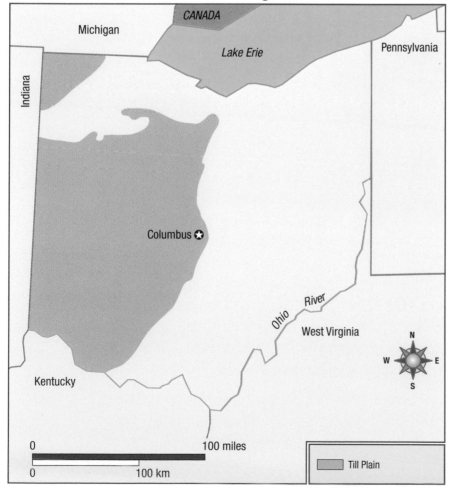

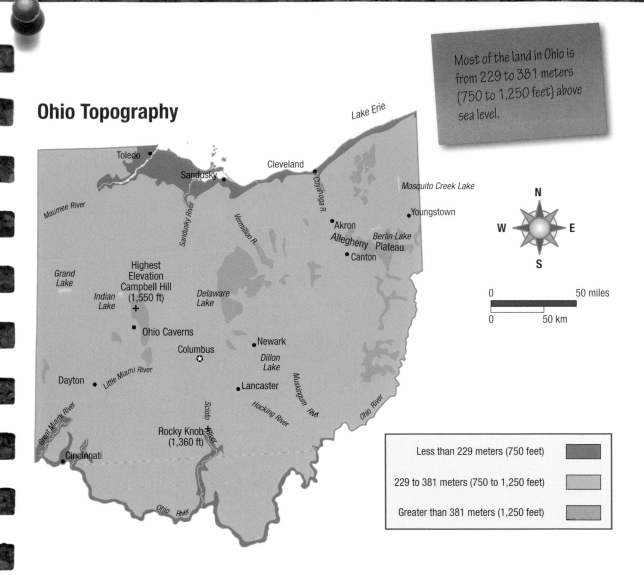

Ohio Topography

Most of the land in Ohio is from 229 to 381 meters (750 to 1,250 feet) above sea level.

Lake Erie

Toledo
Sandusky
Cleveland
Mosquito Creek Lake
Maumee River
Cuyahoga R.
Youngstown
Sandusky River
Akron
Vermillion R.
Allegheny Plateau
Berlin Lake
Canton
Grand Lake
Highest Elevation Campbell Hill (1,550 ft)
Indian Lake
Delaware Lake
Ohio Caverns
Columbus
Newark
Dillon Lake
Dayton
Little Miami River
Lancaster
Muskingum River
Scioto River
Hocking River
Ohio River
Great Miami River
Rocky Knob (1,360 ft)
Cincinnati
Ohio River

N
W   E
S

0   50 miles
0   50 km

Less than 229 meters (750 feet)	
229 to 381 meters (750 to 1,250 feet)	
Greater than 381 meters (1,250 feet)	

Natural Resources

The Ice Age glacier deposited fertile soil called till in this region, which is south of the Black Swamp. After the last Ice Age, the till produced forests that were filled with trees, plants, and animals for many years. When settlers came to Ohio, they cut down most of Ohio's forested land to use the rich soil for farmland that still lies in the Till Plains today. Farmers in this region raise corn, soybeans, wheat, and livestock such as dairy cattle. This region forms the eastern edge of what is called the corn belt, an area of fertile land that runs across a number of Midwestern states.

In the small towns beyond the major cities of the Till Plains, life centers on agriculture. Darke County, on the Indiana border, ranks number one in the state for corn and soybean production. Darke County and Mercer County to its north are also important producers

Ohio is at the edge of what is called the corn belt, making it a leading agricultural state.

To find out more about Ohio's counties, see the map on page 30.

of cattle, poultry, and hogs. Warren County, to the southeast of Darke County, is home to one of the largest goat farms in the United States.

Some tobacco crops grow in Brown, Clermont, and Highland counties. These counties are in the southern part of the Till Plains, where the soil is thinner than in the north of the region. In the southern counties of the Till Plains, there are almost 8,000 farms. They grow corn, wheat, soybeans, hay, and oats. Farmers raise dairy and beef cattle, as well as pigs and sheep.

What Can I Do with a Soybean?

You might be surprised to learn how many uses there are for this tiny golden bean that grows in fields. Crayons, manufactured in northeastern Ohio, are made from soybeans. So is the ink used in printing many newspapers. In the future, you might find soybean paint and auto supplies. Soybeans are already used in many foods, and scientists are developing new uses for them all the time. Look in the grocery store and health food aisles to find soybeans in cooking oil, candy, snacks, and salad dressings. Products manufactured from soybeans are good for you. They contain fiber, calcium, and potassium.

Industry

Large cities in the Till Plains, such as Cincinnati, Dayton, and the state capital, Columbus, are home to international **industries**. Like the Lake Plains, the Till Plains **prospered** from industrial growth, largely driven by strong transportation routes. This region has many types of industries. It relies on the local labor force, or the workers who live in the region.

Columbus is near the exact center of the state. Columbus is the only capital city in the United States that was built especially to be a capital. Early government leaders chose the location because its rivers provided transportation to other cities. A short **canal** joined Columbus to other towns on the Ohio & Erie Canal, and roads to other cities were built. Today, interstates have replaced the slower, older roads.

To find out more about Ohio's transportation, see the map on page 32.

Workers in and around Columbus have different types of jobs. Major employers in the central Ohio area include Honda, a car manufacturer in Marysville that employs 10,000 workers, and the Limited, a clothing manufacturer in Columbus that also employs 10,000 workers.

Columbus links to other **urban** centers through a network of highways. Below, a bridge crosses the Scioto River.

Battelle, also in Columbus, employs more than 7,000 people, many of them scientists and engineers. Battelle develops **technologies** and products for the automotive, **pharmaceutical**, and **agrochemical** industries, as well as for the United States government.

Cincinnati is the state's third largest city, after Columbus and Cleveland. Cincinnati sits on the banks of the Ohio River and connects Ohio with the Mississippi River and the Gulf of Mexico. Cincinnati is Ohio's largest **port** on the Ohio River. Oddly, Cincinnati's airport is across the Ohio River in Kentucky. Interstates carry products made in Cincinnati in every direction.

Spotlight on Delaware

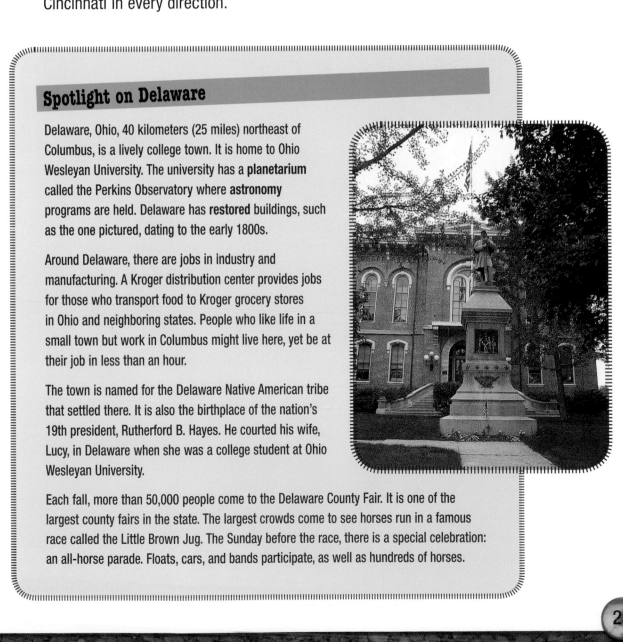

Delaware, Ohio, 40 kilometers (25 miles) northeast of Columbus, is a lively college town. It is home to Ohio Wesleyan University. The university has a **planetarium** called the Perkins Observatory where **astronomy** programs are held. Delaware has **restored** buildings, such as the one pictured, dating to the early 1800s.

Around Delaware, there are jobs in industry and manufacturing. A Kroger distribution center provides jobs for those who transport food to Kroger grocery stores in Ohio and neighboring states. People who like life in a small town but work in Columbus might live here, yet be at their job in less than an hour.

The town is named for the Delaware Native American tribe that settled there. It is also the birthplace of the nation's 19th president, Rutherford B. Hayes. He courted his wife, Lucy, in Delaware when she was a college student at Ohio Wesleyan University.

Each fall, more than 50,000 people come to the Delaware County Fair. It is one of the largest county fairs in the state. The largest crowds come to see horses run in a famous race called the Little Brown Jug. The Sunday before the race, there is a special celebration: an all-horse parade. Floats, cars, and bands participate, as well as hundreds of horses.

The Queen City of the West, as Cincinnati is known, enjoys its riverfront location. Professional sporting events, concerts, and festivals all take place on its riverbank.

Cincinnati, founded in 1788, is home to many of Ohio's industries. Before the Civil War, Cincinnati earned the nickname Porkopolis because it had many pork processing plants. Today, industries in Cincinnati manufacture products you use everyday, such as soaps, detergents, and toothpaste from Proctor & Gamble.

Proctor & Gamble was started by William Proctor, who made candles, and James Gamble, who made soap. The two men married two sisters, Olivia and Elizabeth Norris, and soon combined their skills. During the Civil War (1861–1865), Proctor & Gamble supplied the Union Army with its products.

Proctor & Gamble employs over 14,000 workers in Ohio.

After the war, news of its soap and candles spread. The company expanded and grew. When light bulbs replaced the need for candles, Proctor & Gamble stopped manufacturing candles. Today, the company makes medicine, cleaning products, and even diapers.

Another successful business that started in Cincinnati is Kroger. Barney Kroger started a grocery business in downtown Cincinnati in 1883. It was the first grocery store to have its own bakery. Today, the Kroger Company has more than 2,000 stores in 32 states. It employs 26,000 people in Ohio.

Dayton, to the northeast of Cincinnati, ranks among the top ten largest cities in Ohio. Dayton is known for its great inventors and **unique** industries. The city's founders thought that building the city where the Stillwater, Mad, and Great Miami rivers met would help it grow. They were right, but whenever the rivers flooded, Dayton became a muddy mess. The flood of 1913 was the worst in Ohio's history. Afterward, a series of dams were built to stop flooding disasters.

Football Factories

If you are a football fan, you have probably seen touchdowns made with a Wilson brand football. In fact, every point ever scored by players in the National Football League (NFL) was scored with an Ohio-made football. The Wilson Football Factory in Ada, Ohio, manufactures footballs for high schools and colleges, as well as for professional and youth teams of all ages. Workers make 5,000 footballs a day.

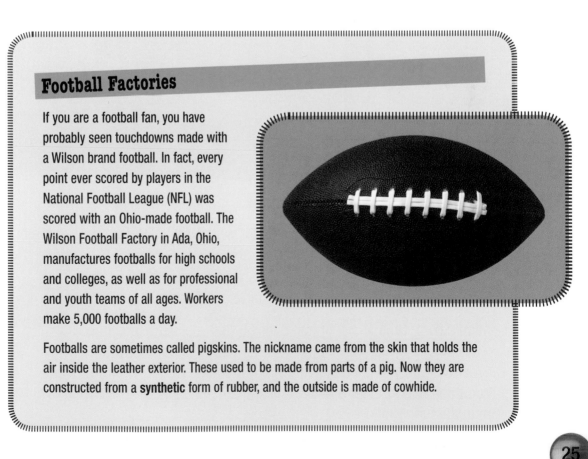

Footballs are sometimes called pigskins. The nickname came from the skin that holds the air inside the leather exterior. These used to be made from parts of a pig. Now they are constructed from a **synthetic** form of rubber, and the outside is made of cowhide.

The Wright brothers, inventors of the airplane, lived in Dayton. After their first successful flight, Dayton became, and still is, a center for flight-related industries. Flight companies employ thousands of scientists, engineers, and technicians. Wright-Patterson Air Force Base, for example, supplies important research for the United States Air Force and is one of Ohio's top five employers. It employs over 22,000 Ohioans.

Wright-Patterson Air Force Base is located near Dayton and employs many Ohioans.

Charles Kettering was another inventor who lived in Dayton. He invented the electric cash register and the electric starter for cars. Mr. Kettering's inventions brought shopping and driving to a new level. National Cash Register (NCR) has its world headquarters in Dayton.

Middletown, Ohio, a city of just over 50,000 residents, became well-known for its steel industry in the early 1900s. Today, the AK Steel Company in Middletown employs almost 10,000 workers. The company makes steel products for the automobile, construction, and manufacturing industries.

Education

Many outstanding colleges and universities, as well as fine public school systems, are located in the Till Plains. They employ many workers besides offering courses for thousands of students.

Near Dayton, you will find one of the oldest private African-American universities in the United States. Called Wilberforce University, it is located in the small city of Wilberforce. This city has a rich **Underground Railroad** history.

The city of Wilberforce is also the home of Central State University. It is a state university which has a mostly African-American student body and professors. The National Afro-American Museum & Cultural Center is located near both of the universities in Wilberforce. Exhibits at the museum often tell stories of African Americans who lived in Ohio and elsewhere in the world.

The mission of the National Afro-American Museum & Cultural Center is to educate the public about African-American history and culture.

Ohio State University has one of the largest **campuses** in the United States. It is based in Columbus, but has campuses all around Ohio. Ohio State University opened in 1870 as the Ohio Agricultural and Mechanical College. Today, it is a huge university with almost 60,000 students.

Ohio State University offers around 12,000 different courses at its campuses.

Climate

The **climate** in the Till Plains is more moderate than in northern regions. On average, temperatures are higher and snowfall is lower, but there have been damaging weather patterns here, too. Rivers, including the mighty Ohio River, often flood their banks. More than 450 people lost their lives when the Great Miami and Scioto rivers flooded in 1913, and more than 250 people died in the 1937 Ohio River flood.

Tornadoes struck Xenia, north of Cincinnati, not once, but twice—in 1974 and again in 2000. This part of Ohio is part of Tornado Alley, a region where many tornadoes are likely to take place. Meteorologists, scientists who study weather patterns, say there are often tornado weather conditions here.

Flooding along the Ohio River is an occasional threat, as seen in this photo of flooding in Cincinnati in 1997.

Glaciated Plateau

The Appalachian **Plateau** has some of Ohio's most **dramatic** scenery, including waterfalls, cliffs, and sandstone rock formations. The area known as the Glaciated Appalachian Plateau lies north of the Unglaciated Appalachian Plateau. Except for the narrow strip along the Lake Erie shore where the Lake Plains lie, the Glaciated Plateau covers northeastern Ohio in a bent-knee shape down to a point past the center of the state.

This region includes cities such as Akron, Canton, Mansfield, and Youngtown. When put together with Cleveland and other cities along Lake Erie, it is the most populated and **prosperous** area of the state.

Glaciated Plateau Region

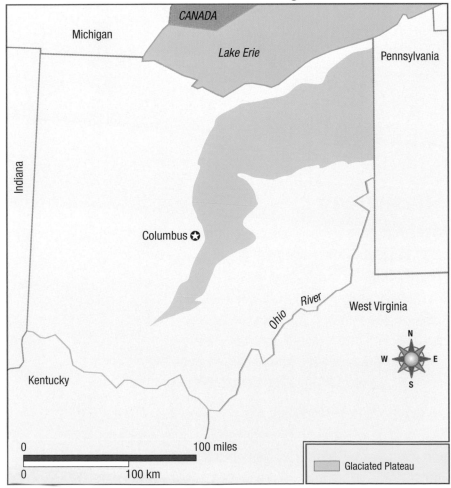

Ohio Population Density by County, 2000

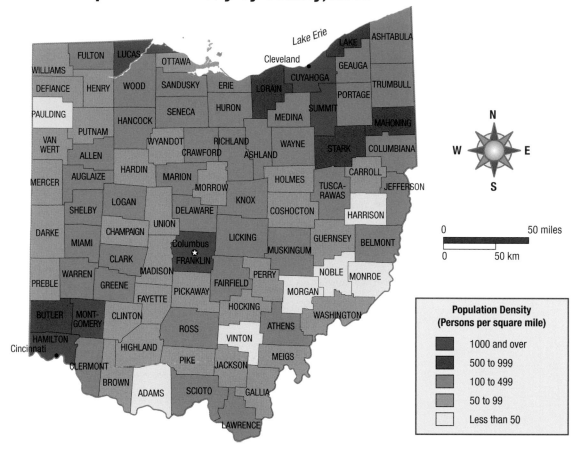

Population Density
(Persons per square mile)

- 1000 and over
- 500 to 999
- 100 to 499
- 50 to 99
- Less than 50

Natural Resources

Rich **natural resources**, such as coal, are common in the Glaciated **Plateau**. However, most of the land in this region is fertile farmland. Many of Ohio's **Amish** communities settled in the Glaciated Plateau because of the rich soil covering the gently rolling hills and valleys. They stayed here because the region reminded them of their homelands in Switzerland and Germany, where they lived before they moved to the United States.

The Glaciated Plateau's rich farmlands make it is an important area for raising beef and dairy cattle. It produces many dairy products such as cheese and ice cream. Ohio ranks sixth in the nation for **sherbet** production. Most dairy farms in Ohio are in this region.

To find out more about Ohio's resources, see the map on page 9.

Rich soil left by the glacier that once covered Ohio makes the Glaciated Plateau a strong farming center today.

Ohio grows many flowers and potted plants, which are grown in greenhouses. The **climate** in northeastern Ohio is good for growing grapes, too. The grapes are used to make grape juice and wine. Rows of grape vines line the roads throughout the region. Many apple orchards are found in the area.

Once discovered, coal supplied the energy to run factories here. The large amount of natural resources, with Lake Erie and strong transportation routes nearby, meant that this part of Ohio became another ideal place in Ohio to build factories. To this day, **industries** thrive in the region.

Milk from dairy cattle is the most important farm product in three Glaciated Plateau counties: Ashtabula, Ashland, and Columbiana.

Transportation

By 1820 Ohio's population had grown to 580,000 residents. The main industry of the state at that time was agriculture. But there was no reliable transportation system to move the products produced in Ohio to markets in the East. **Canals** were built to transport goods produced in the Glaciated Plateau to Cleveland and then to **ports** on the Lake Erie coast. The first portion of the Ohio & Erie Canal, linking Akron and Cleveland, was completed in 1827. Later, the canal ran for 495.7 kilometers (308 miles), all the way to the Ohio River.

Railroads were built soon after the canals. Railroads transported many of the products produced in the Glaciated Plateau and other regions of Ohio. Ohio still has railroads, but it used to have a lot more. At one time, more than ten rail lines ran through the Akron area. By 1890 Ohio was a maze of railroads moving north and south, east and west.

Ohio Transportation

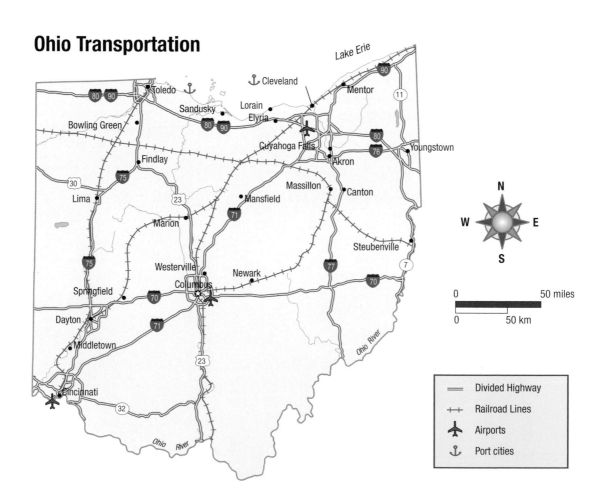

Today, there are only a few railroads left, such as Norfolk-Southern, the new Wheeling & Lake Erie, and the Akron and Barberton Cluster. These, plus Ohio's highways and waterways, add to Ohio's importance as a major transportation crossroads for the whole United States.

Industry

Transportation routes had much to do with the settling of the Glaciated Plateau region of Ohio. As people moved westward across the country, they looked for jobs. Transportation both brought workers and **raw materials** to Ohio cities, and many factories were started. By 1920 factories dotted the northern part of the Glaciated Plateau. They manufactured iron and steel, glass, rubber, automobiles, ships, chemicals, foods products, household products, and hundreds of other items. Today, the area remains one of the largest and most concentrated industrial zones on Earth.

Halls of Fame in Ohio include the Rock and Roll Hall of Fame and Museum in Cleveland; the Pro Football Hall of Fame in Canton; and the Inventors Hall of Fame in Akron (pictured above).

The city of Akron, for example, is known for its plastics and rubber industries. Akron is called the rubber capital of the world. It received this title in the early 1900s. Harvey Firestone began manufacturing tires in Akron for Henry Ford's automobiles in 1905. Akron's population was then around 42,620 people. By 1920, after the Goodyear, Goodrich, and General Tire Companies started, Akron's population numbered more than 200,000 people. Most of them made their living in some way connected with the rubber industry. Although many of the rubber factories have closed, Akron remains the world headquarters of the Goodyear Tire and Rubber Company. Companies in the Glaciated Plateau today have developed new industries, such as the plastics and **polymer** industries. In fact, scientists in Akron have created the ingredient that is used to make almost all plastic children's toys. The Edison Polymer Innovation Corporation in Akron helps companies that make plastics and polymer.

Part of the reason why this region has so many industries is its location. Around four out of every ten people living in the United States and Canada are within 805 kilometers (500 miles) of the region. This means they are within one day's drive. This makes it an ideal location for factories to ship goods to markets in the United States and Canada.

Climate

The Glaciated Plateau is located in what is called the snow belt. There is usually more snow in this region than anywhere else in the state. This is partly because of Lake Erie. During the summer, cool lake breezes provide natural air-conditioning. In the spring, temperatures are cooler and there is more rain than in other regions of Ohio. Also, there is no natural barrier to block cold winds from the north. This means that the winter weather can get very cold in this region.

Winter **recreation** and sports thrive in the Glaciated Plateau region of Ohio.

Ohio's Worst Blizzard

An extreme example of how bad the weather can get in the Glaciated Plateau came on January 26, 1978, in the form of a blizzard. The blizzard began during the night, and when it ended two days later there were 1.2 meters (4 feet) of snow on the ground. Schools across Ohio closed. Some were closed for a whole week. With the snow came winds reaching 113 kilometers (70 miles) per hour. The heavy snowfall and high winds left snow drifts as tall as twenty feet. Driving and shoveling were impossible in some places. Cars and trucks were buried.

The Ohio National Guard helped clear the roads and rescue stranded drivers. President Jimmy Carter announced that Ohio was in a state of emergency. Workers, stranded at their jobs, worked long hours and could not be relieved because of the hazardous road conditions. Volunteers who had cars with four-wheel drive helped transport doctors, nurses, and patients to hospitals. In remote areas where people could not walk to the store, bread was dropped to the ground by helicopters. The American Red Cross and the United States Coast Guard were called to help those in need.

Unglaciated Plateau

The Unglaciated Appalachian **Plateau**, to the south of the Glaciated Appalachian Plateau, looks much different from the rest of Ohio, because the **Ice Age** glaciers did not reach this part of the state. The region, which makes up most of southeastern Ohio, is known for its huge sandstone rocks, caves, **unique** natural rock bridges, and hemlock trees (a tall type of evergreen).

Because of the rough and rugged land in this region, farming is not good. There are few **industries**. Twenty-nine counties in this region and part of the Glaciated Plateau region are called **Appalachia**. They are rich in scenery and beauty, and outdoor activities such as hiking and wildlife watching are popular.

Unglaciated Plateau Region

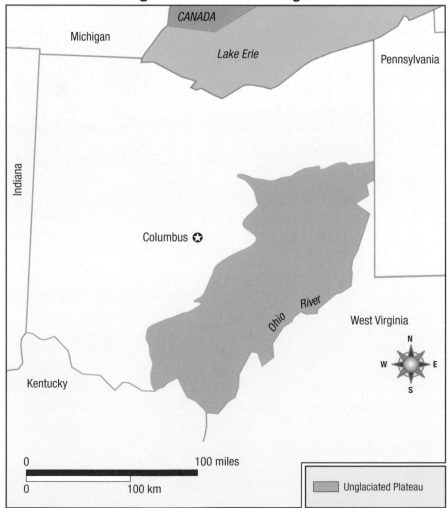

CANADA

Michigan

Lake Erie

Pennsylvania

Indiana

Columbus ✪

Ohio River

West Virginia

N
W — E
S

Kentucky

0   100 miles

0   100 km

    Unglaciated Plateau

The features of Hocking Hills, such as Old Man's Cave, pictured above, are made of sandstone that is more than 350 million years old.

Near the city of Logan, in Hocking County, the Hocking Hills area is among the most **scenic** spots in Ohio. There are hilly trails, and also short, flat trails leading to waterfalls and cliff views. Hocking Hills State Park is the place to find unusual rock formations, like caves and natural rock bridges. During winter, when the temperatures are cold enough, the waterfalls freeze.

This part of Ohio may be rich in natural beauty, but it is the poorest **economic** region in the state. All the counties in the Unglaciated Plateau receive financial help from the government. Most communities in this region are rural. There are few major cities, big businesses, or industries. The area lacks the economic advantages found in other places in the state of Ohio today.

Using Resources

Ice Age glaciers stopped before they reached this region, so they could not deposit or leave behind any fertile soil here. They also stopped before flattening out the region's hills, and it is difficult to grow crops on land that is not flat.

Despite these conditions, some unique types of farming take place in the region. Farmers take pride in growing small quantities of homegrown products, often sold in small markets. They raise livestock, including beef and dairy cattle. They also grow unusual crops like paw-paw plants used for making jams and herbs that are considered naturally healing medicines.

Tobacco is an important crop in the southern part of the region. It grows in fields along the Ohio River. Crops are dried in tobacco barns with big open windows that allow the air to move around inside. Tobacco barns do not look like livestock barns. Tobacco barns have large doors and windows. The tobacco leaves hang inside in neat rows. When the harvest is ready, it is sold at auction.

Inside this tobacco barn in southern Ohio, tobacco leaves hang in rows in order to dry out. When they are ready, they will be sold at an auction.

One of the largest cities in Ohio's Unglaciated Plateau is Zanesville. About 113 kilometers (70 miles) east of Columbus, the city of Zanesville sits on the banks of the Muskingum River. It has a population of more than 25,000 people. Zanesville was once known as Clay City. It has also been called the Pottery Capital of the World. Its rich history in the production of pottery began over 100 years ago. The Zanesville pottery industry still exists to this day and pottery factories continue to employ hundreds of local residents.

Zanesville, known for its pottery history is also famous for its Y-shaped bridge, one of few that exist worldwide.

Industry

There are few big industries in the Unglaciated Plateau today, but this region was important to the growth of Ohio hundreds of years ago. Some children living in Appalachia are **descendants** of Native Americans and Europeans who lived in this hilly region more than 200 years ago. The grandfathers and great-grandfathers of these children may have worked in the coal and **iron ore** mines. The miners helped Ohio grow during the time of the **Industrial Era**.

During the Industrial Era, Ohio's forests became overused. Today, Ohioans are working to grow forests again.

Settlers chopped and cleared forests throughout Ohio to create communities and farms. These forests became fuel for Ohio's major iron industry in the Unglaciated Plateau region. One area, called Hanging Rock, at the southern tip of the state, was famous for its charcoal iron furnaces. Workers produced charcoal from the wood. Charcoal heated the furnaces. Workers poured the hot liquid iron into rectangle-shaped molds called *pigs*. They named the iron rectangles pig iron. Pig iron was used to manufacture other iron products.

The furnaces helped Ohio grow into a strong industrial state. The owners of the furnaces hired many workers. Some of the workers mined the iron ore. Others built and operated furnaces. Still others chopped trees and made charcoal, or built roads to haul limestone, another resource used in iron production. When the resources in one area were used up, everyone moved to another spot and started the process all over again.

Mines in Appalachia are part of Ohio's past, but they were necessary to make Ohio the state it is today.

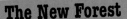

The towns that formed around iron production were called company towns, because everyone who lived there worked for the same company. The iron companies owned thousands of acres of land rich in **natural resources**. But eventually they used up the region's resources and closed down.

Today, the iron furnaces and the huge iron industry that contributed so much to Ohio are part of the state's past. Visitors can see how the iron furnaces worked at Buckeye Furnace in Jackson County. It has a **restored** copy of the original furnace dating from 1852. The original closed in 1894, but parts of the old furnace are still there. It is managed by the Ohio Historical Society. The former company store is now a visitors' center.

Transportation

Many people who make their home in river towns along the mighty Ohio River spend their spare time on the river or along the shore. They watch for passing **barges**, **ferryboats**, and riverboats. The Ohio River, like Lake Erie to the north, helped Ohio grow over the past 200 years. Freighters carry a variety of products, such as coal, grains, and gravel by the ton to markets all over the world.

Occasionally, the Ohio River floods. Some buildings are still standing along the shore with watermarks up to the second floor bedrooms. People living in 1937 still tell stories about the Ohio River's worst flood. More than 250 people lost their lives during this national disaster.

Marietta, Ohio's First European Town

Marietta, an energetic river town, is located along the banks of the Muskingum River and the Ohio River in the Unglaciated Plateau. It is famous in Ohio history because it was the first organized settlement in the **Northwest Territory**. It has changed over the years, but it remains a charming example of what life is like along the Ohio River. People there like to watch activity along the river from park benches or on a blanket on the riverbank.

Marietta is a modern city, but each September the annual **Sternwheeler** Festival reminds Ohioans of the large boats with big paddle wheels that were once the grandest way to travel. Passengers' favorite overnight spot was the Historic Lafayette Hotel. It was built in 1918 and still serves as Marietta's major hotel. It overlooks the point, a favorite docking spot, along the river. The hotel was named for one of Marietta's first visitors, the Marquis de Lafayette, who stopped there in 1825.

Bluegrass

The Bluegrass is Ohio's smallest **landform** region. It is a tiny triangular region along the Ohio River. It gets its name from Kentucky, where the Bluegrass region continues to the south. This region consists of hilly and gently rolling land. The Bluegrass region makes up most of Adams County.

Like the Unglaciated Appalachian **Plateau**, the Bluegrass region was not covered with the **Ice Age** glacier. Thus, the soil in the Bluegrass is thin, and only slightly more fertile than soil in the Unglaciated Plateau to the north and east. This is because the soils in the Bluegrass are based on a bedrock of limestone and shale.

Bluegrass Region

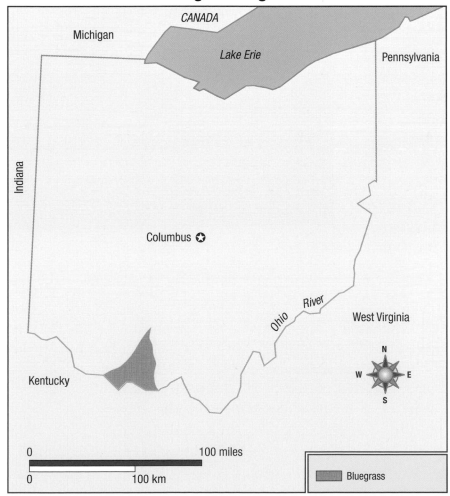

Ohio's Bluegrass region extends into the heart of Kentucky, the state which borders Ohio to the south.

Adams County is mainly known for the wide variety of prairie plants and bluegrass found there. Bluegrass is not actually blue, but is green with a white flower. The area has a small farming **industry**, but it does not contribute much to the **economy** of Ohio. Adams County has less than 50 people per square mile, making it one of the most rural counties in the state.

There are just a handful of other counties in Ohio with such a small population. These are mainly in the Unglaciated Plateau region. Without industries to provide jobs for large numbers of people, the population of the Bluegrass region, like that of the Unglaciated Plateau, remains small.

All around Ohio, it is people that make it into the successful industrial state that it is today. People provide the labor to create the products that contribute to Ohio's economy. People use Ohio's **natural resources** to produce goods and services. They also use them for **recreation**, for play as well as work. Ohio may look different today than it did to its first residents, but people still live in the state for many of the same reasons: the resources of the land, jobs, and quality of life.

Map of Ohio

Ohio

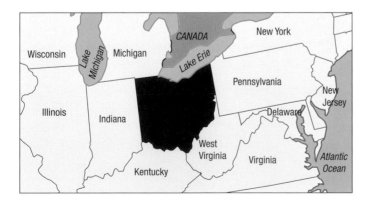

Glossary

agrochemical chemical used to kill insects and plants that are harmful to crops

Amish followers of Jacob Amman, a strict Mennonite of the 1600s, who settled in America in the 1700s

Appalachia twenty-nine counties in southeastern Ohio that form most of the Appalachian Plateau

astronomy science of the planets and outer space

barge broad boat with a flat bottom used on rivers and canals

campus grounds and buildings of a university or school

canal human-made waterway

census official count of the number of people living in a certain place

climate weather conditions that are usual for a certain area

dense having parts that are crowded together; thick

descendant person born of a certain family or group

dramatic lively

dredge remove earth

economy system of managing the production, distribution, and use of goods and services

ferryboat type of boat that carries people over small bodies of water

flint type of hard stone used by Paleo-Indians to make weapons and tools

gorge narrow steep-walled canyon or part of a canyon

Great Lakes five lakes—Superior, Michigan, Huron, Erie, and Ontario—that lie in the northern United States and southern Canada

gross domestic product value of the total amount of goods and services produced by the people in a state during a certain time

high-tech having to do with technology and computers. High-tech is short for the term high-technology.

human resource person who works to create goods or services

Ice Age period of colder climate when thick glaciers covered much of the land. The last Ice Age ended about 11,500 years ago.

Industrial Era period of the 1800s to early 1900s during which industries overtook farming as the main source of jobs

industrialist person who owns or manages a type of industry

industry manufacturing activity; group of businesses that offer a similar product or service. Things having to do with industry are called industrial.

iron ore mineral mined for the iron it contains

landform natural feature of the land surface

Mennonite Christian religion characterized by simplicity of life and unwillingness to fight

NASA National Air and Space Administration

natural resource something from nature that can be useful to humans

Northwest Territory historic region of the United States that was split into the present-day states of Ohio, Indiana, Illinois, Michigan, Wisconsin, and part of Minnesota

pharmaceutical having to do with medication

planetarium building in which images of planets and stars are projected onto a domed ceiling

plateau broad flat area of high land

polar relating to the cold regions of the North or South Pole

political boundary landform or imaginary line that separates two places with different governments, such as counties, states, or countries

polymer human-made material used in making all kinds of goods, from rubber soles to stuffed toys to the bristles on a toothbrush

port place where ships load and unload cargo

prehistoric relating to a time before recorded or spoken history

prosper success in making money

raw material material in its natural condition that is used to produce goods

recreation means of refreshing the mind and body; fun

reservoir place where water is kept for future use

restore bring back to an original state

scenic giving views of natural places

sherbet fruity frozen dessert made with milk or egg white

sternwheeler steam boat driven by a large paddle wheel at the rear of the boat

suburb city or town just outside a larger city. Things having to do with a suburb are called suburban.

synthetic made or produced by human beings, usually by chemical means; artificial

technology using science to find solutions

terminal station from which trains or planes depart and enter

Underground Railroad system of cooperation by people opposed to slavery in the United States before 1863, by which runaway slaves were secretly helped to reach freedom

unique one of a kind

urban having to do with the city

wetland very wet, low-lying land

Find Out More

Books

Brown, Jonathan A. and Frances Ruffin. *Ohio*. Strongsville, OH: Gareth Stevens, 2006.

Curry, Judson and Elizabeth Curry. *Regions of the USA: The Midwest*. Chicago: Raintree, 2007.

McHugh, Erin. *Ohio*. New York: Black Dog and Leventhal Publishers, 2007.

Stille, Darlene R. *Ohio*. Danbury, CT: Children's Press, 2008.

Website

http://www.dnr.state.oh.us/

The Ohio Department of Natural Resources provides information about the state's forests, nature preserves, and parks. It also has a list of Ohio's endangered species.

Index